Alone with the Terrible Universe

by

Alan Britt

CypressBooks
Rio Rico, Arizona

CypressBooks

CypressBooks
Rio Rico, AZ
USA

Taya M. Graham and Joanne Bracken, Editorial Assistants

Page Layout & Design by Rodney J. Urand

Cover Design by Sequel Design: www.sequeldesign.com

Cover painting by José Rodeiro: "9/11"...Oil-on canvas (2001)...36" x 48" Collection of the artist:: www.rodeiro-art.com

Cover painting photograph by Charles P. Hayes

ISBN-10: #0-9647754-7-6
ISBN-13: #978-0-9647754-7-3

Library of Congress Control Number: 2010917756

Manufactured in the United States of America.

Printed by McNaughton & Gunn, Inc.
Saline, MI.

10 9 8 7 6 5 4 3 2 1

Alone with the Terrible Universe

ACKNOWLEDGEMENTS

Grateful acknowledgement to the editors of publications in which the following poems appeared:

Ann Arbor Review: "Palomino Leaves," "Solitude," and "Wednesday"

Ascent Aspirations Magazine (Canada): "March Dream"

Autumn Sky Poetry: "Solitude in a Park in Thurmont, Maryland"

The Bergen Street Review: "Green Oxygen"

Best Poem: "Sundown"

The Bitter Oleander: "Irony," and "Unit One: Our Relationship to the Universe"

BlazeVOX: "Spring's Interference," "Bitten," "A Rainy Thursday Afternoon," and "Rattan Fans Circle the Ceiling"

Blue Fifth Review: "Idea that Became a Creatury"

Bolts of Silk (Scotland): "April Afternoon"

ByLine: "Return to Teaching"

Cider Press Review: "November 30, 2001"

English Journal: "September, 2001," and "Reisterstown, October, 2001"

Eskimo Pie: "The Corpse," "The Stars," "Myth," "Driving to School," "September Lament," and "Australian Shiraz"

Exercise Bowler: "Monday Evening," and "After a Storm"

Flutter Poetry Journal: "April Birds," and "Curious Universe"

Fullosia Press: "Fee Fie Foe Fum," "September Lament," "Marrying Myths," "October Dogs," "Halloween, 2001," "Thanksgiving Eve," "November Morning," "On Dealing with Fate," "December, 2001," "Happy Holidays!," "April Dusk," and "Twilight"

Futures Mysterious Anthology Magazine: "Christmas, 2001," and "December Sun"

The Great American Poetry Show 2: "The Old Toad"

Hecale (United Kingdom): "Birds of the Universe Congregate in Reisterstown"

Illogical Muse: "June Evening"

Illya's Honey: "Barbequing, Christmas, 2001"

Ken*again: "An Early, California Merlot," "Wild Parrots," "Twilight," and "Chilly Summer Dusk"

The Legendary: "The Day Alice Came By," "Holiday from Teaching," and "My Companion and I Listen to Paco de Lucia Play *Solo Quiero Caminar*"

Mad Swirl (The Poetry Forum): "Childhood"

Meridian Anthology of Contemporary Poetry: "Driving to School," and "Cockatiel"

Long Island Quarterly: "Coral Voice"

Pidjin: "Pleasure Dome," "September, 2001," and "Unit One: Our Relationship to the Universe"

The Recusant (United Kingdom): "Listening to Roy Buchanan's *Peter Gunn*"

River Oak Review: "Dark Matter"

Shoots and Vines: "Tragic Hero," "Another Evening, Possibly in

December, as I Recall," "Ode to Ether," "Four Birds," "Late Afternoon Wine," and "March Afternoon"

Skyline Literary Magazine: "Love Poem," "White Thursday," "June Evening," and "Love Poem"

Square Lake: "Alone with the Terrible Universe," "Anxious Autumn," and "Australian Merlot"

Strangeroad: "Poems in Progress," "Here's to Writing a Poem on the 13th of Every Month for an Entire Year, but Knowing I'd Never Remember All That..." and "Twilight"

The Underwood Review: "Thoreau Says We Must Live Within Two Miles of Our Primary Childhood," and "Chilly Summer Dusk"

Unlikely 2.0: "Tuesday Before Thanksgiving," "The Day After," and "On Dealing with Fate"

Yellow Mama: " Friday, March 8, 2002," and "House Finches"

* * * * * *

"June Evening" appeared in *The Best of Illogical Muse 2008*, Amber Rothrock, Editor, Buchanan, MI: 2008.

"September 11, 2001" appeared in *International Gallerie: Poetry in Art/Art in Poetry Issue*, v13 No.2 (India)Bina Sarkar Ellias, Editor, Mumbai, India: 2010.

* * * * * *

Jose Rodeiro's painting *9/11* appeared in *International Gallerie: Poetry in Art/Art in Poetry Issue*, v13 No.2 (India)Bina Sarkar Ellias, Editor, Mumbai, India: 2010.

CONTENTS

Part I

Part II

Part III

Part IV

Part V

About the book

Alone with the Terrible Universe began in September 2001. The first two poems are indicative of where the manuscript might have gone, but then September 11th. From that point forward, ending June the following year, a cycle of poems grew like an anti-garden. The idea was to keep the garden devoid of sentimentality, that sweetest of illusions, at all times. With ebbs and flows these poems absorbed the undercurrents of the next nine months.

--Alan Britt

Part I

She'd sit, deep in her thoughts, upon a park banquette —

To listen to those concerts, heavy in the brasses,
With which the military sometimes floods our parks,
And which, on golden evenings when life effervesces,
Pour heroism into all good people's hearts.

She'd sit, always erect, distinguished, almost regal,
Inhaling brisk and warlike tunes with every breath;
Her eye would open like the eye of an old eagle;
Her alabaster brow deserved a laurel wreath.

--Charles Baudelaire

The Corpse

A corpse swings
in a web,
where hemotoxins
and neurotoxins
deliver dreams of rotting moons
tossed like old cabbages
into the holds
of tiny ships filled to capacity
sailing across an ocean
of blood.

The corpse is ancient.

Crickets,
embedded,
flicker magnesium.

The Stars

The stars are shamans.

They paint arroyos
the color
of Gilas:
bruised-orange,
black,
burnt-ochre.

Sand
flows through
the universe's thin waist,
emerges
from
cottonwood's
three hips
shaped
like
green
mantras.

Alone with the Terrible Universe

My shadow
attacks
the cedar
lattice
that surrounds
the patio.

Lamplight
flickering thick September maples
splotches
the muscular cedar boards.

A dog,
a small brown and white
dog barks
across a dark sea
of crickets
all hunched together
like millions of glistening coquina shells
on a black shore.

Return to Teaching

Today I got to write
Federico García Lorca's name
on a green chalkboard!

So, the proof of my madness
is the dust on my fingertips
from a luna moth's struggling wings?

Anyway, today, I got to write
Federico García Lorca's name
on a green chalkboard!

September 11, 2001

(The diameter of the bomb was thirty centimeters.)
                  --Yehuda Amichai

The question is,
the bomb was half the size
of the propane tank
hanging from your barbeque grill;
so, how vast is the mourning
that gradually ascends the sleepy darkness
of an innocent night?

Ripples of grief,
tailpipe tears
of refined oil
colliding
with bloody ripples
from Jerusalem, Algiers, the Sudan,
Kosovo, Northern Ireland, Bogotá,
and, today, Manhattan Island, that lusty landscape,
once Walt Whitman's muscular dream of hope,
now García Lorca's toxic nightmare.

So, the question remains,
the bomb was half the size
of the propane tank
hanging from your red barbeque grill,
thus, leading to one simple question:
Just how vast is the mourning
that gradually ascends the sleepy darkness
of an innocent night?

Myth

The King had many opportunities
to blunder big time.

After all, it took a whole month
for news
to travel
anywhere,
much less
across a border.

That's plenty of time
to cover your tracks.

So, imagine
that life as a monarch
or a pharaoh
agrees with your sultry disposition.

But, also remember, one night when you're dreaming
about wine
and scarab-eyed women
with shaman hips,
as Federico predicted,
several large black crickets
could easily devour you
at a moment's notice.

And on that very night,
golden porch light
squeezing diamonds
through patio lattice

will resemble
the fur of an ocelot.

Pleasure Dome

That squirrel's nest, twenty-two feet above
my left shoulder,
tobacco-colored twigs and leaves
stacked high,
almost enough to fill
a small wheelbarrow.

This happens to be the perfect maple
for residence
since the main trunk lists
far to the right
creating a cool umbrella
of muscular green.

A gray and white cat
scampers through the damp waist
of late afternoon.

Echoes
of cars
paste
the sky.

Driving to School

On our neighborhood street
this fawn
faces me half a block away
then vaporizes down a drainage ditch
through misty predawn humidity.

As I pass by
a *second* fawn's slender whitetail
like a moonlit metronome
washes the drainage ditch's
wet grey concrete.

Fee Fie Foe Fum

The US, an oil
sucking giant,
removes its dipstick
from the starving
throats of Afghan refugees,
whose necks
like hungry birds
extend
from canvas huts.

We're a quart and a half low,
says the President
(Republican or Democrat).

Must be time
to replace the King.

September, 2001

September has thick, emerald hair,
a thin waist of traffic,
and a distant white dog
gnawing the first hour of late afternoon.

September has seen buildings crumble,
grief worn like scarves.

The large body of October
already rises up
through yellow leaves
with tiny capillaries
slowed to a crawl
by a sudden Canadian chill.

September leans on a split-rail fence
and watches yellow leaves
sail by in a swirling gust of ashes.

Anxious Autumn

A bushy gray dog
laps the caws of crows
like ice chips
from the frozen horizon.

A young girl
steps from the 8th grade
to practice her diamond sensitive poems
for tomorrow's Bat Mitzvahs.

The crows, black spearheads
threading wild forsythia.

Forsythia speaks:
It is wise to serve despair
not only with a liberal helping
of mashed potatoes,
gravy, if you like,
but also with a generous fist of black pepper,
thereby stimulating intelligence
from this beastly emotion.

Australian Merlot

The label says merlot,
but I swear it has that
wooden ambiance
more closely associated with cabernet.

Fire engines clot
our neighborhood street,
the fluttering artery
of the bourgeoisie.

Black dogs bark at the gate
as ashes of souls and asbestos
rain down on the neighborhoods.

September Lament

I'm trying to win the mind back,
snatching it from the jaws
of capitalist behavior.

Democracy was once a thirsty canoe
launched upon a philosophy of indigenous dreams
and wild rivers to nourish
the body of free society.

But now the white gloves of industry
are the ones spewing Maserati smoke
to obscure the scalping of entire nations.

I'm telling you,
despite chips falling
from the torso of a marble Venus,
there's a complex web
of imagination
expanding at an alarming rate
in the crawl spaces
of our split-level lives.

Irony

We squander
precious minutes
from our lives every day
in convenience stores,
at gas pumps,
or trapped between the mink eyelashes
of the local news anchor woman.

However, if we're lucky,
a few authentic moments trickle
from the gaping wounds
of a suffering Bartok violin.

Occasionally, some rare moments get pounded
into millet
for paintings that sag
below white shadows
in the Louvre.

But, tonight, all these minutes
are strung together
like a chorus of crickets
into a necklace
of burning jetliners
around the smooth neck
of a mourning dove.

Idea that Became a Creature

Is this about an idea
that became a creature?

Not exactly.

But I thought…

That's well documented.
Your theories have sashayed
like dust devils
through the empty halls
of academia
for millennia.
But now it's time
to place your brain
in a hammock,
a chrysalis,
if you like,
but a swaying reality,
nonetheless.

And after you release your gaze
from the largest hornet's nest
this side of these desperately proud Mid-Atlantic states,
we'll visit
a vivid
yellow and black
garden spider
hovering in the breeze
barely a nervous twitch
from her two thousand

and one
quivering eggs.

Australian Shiraz

Fruit flies attempt to romance
this shapely, brunette shiraz.

She's tempting.

But, alas, the hand of fate
waves us all away.

So, I huddle
below early autumn fireflies
whose exhausted lime bodies
flicker momentary myths and naïve German fables.

Eventually, my severe gazes
send tracers of dotted green light
through night's tin roof
dusted by glistening, cocktail-lounge stars.

Nothing much to live for,
I suppose,
since fate has cultivated
more
than a casual infatuation
for my ruby-hipped,
bare-shouldered,
brunette shiraz.

Part II

First, God made idiots.
Then he made school boards.

--Samuel Clemens

Autumn

*

I believe that manna
was originally meant for banana.

**

Death hops the rickety running boards
of Emily's chariot to peek over
the dusty shoulders
of every programmer
at her cubicle.

***

In West Palm Beach,
August steam rising
from early morning blacktops
of my brother's adolescence
cultivated fists
of disenchanted life.

****

Some flags that burned
for generations
now resemble
red and white feathers
knotted against a herd
of flowing, blueblack
Apache hair.

Marrying Myths

(We want to put his ass in the stir!
We want to pin this triple murder
on him, he ain't no Gentleman Jim!)
                --Bob Dylan

I married a myth.
She drifted away.

I awoke
in the throat of a gold mine.

Hurricane Carter paid dearly
for his myth,
a myth spread by pallet knives
across the blemished forehead of Democracy,
a myth complicated by age-old extortion and bigotry.

But, tonight, I feel like dreaming
a new myth,
one with hips
of black wine,
one whose kisses resemble rainbirds
in shiny long black coats
strolling like stately gods of pepper
over St. Croix's windy white sand
strewn with bruised yellow
and green palm fronds.

A brand new myth,
one that takes the mystery
out of satellites

prowling much too high
above our clouds of freedom.

Unit One: Our Relationship
to the Universe

Chilly solitude
or an orgiastic conventional life?

I made my announcement
with a badly stained,
loose fitting, yellow slipper,
the one with a tiny crack
in the center
of its vinyl sole
violently snagging
a rubber-tipped
spring wall protector
at the bottom
of our patio door.

But this patio door leads to darkness,
Mediterranean blue clouds,
plus the ochre smear
across a pear balanced on angle
in a Cezanne still life.

The pear opens its sliding patio door
and announces to the universe
that I am
its honorable guest for the evening.

For One Moment, and One Moment Only, I Escape the Petty World, the Teal-Patterned Silk Noose Choking Human Ego, and Heavy Clumps of Bureaucracy Stuck to False Eyelashes

I float above
a veranda
of twisted, elephant roots.

Streetlamp's whiteblue face
shivers
in a brief
October breeze.

Hunched, yellow
maple leaves
dream inside
blistering cicadas.

October Garden in Maryland

Green tomatoes
beg
to be left alone.

They droop,
talk in
whispers,
caress
each others'
hollow tubes.

Two golden tomatoes
in the back row,
translucent
large drops
of yellow
metamorphic
dozing tears.

A whitened wood stake
crippled
to the right.

Holding firm,
one orangered
beauty:
stark reality.

Watching Two Squirrels

Hips of wine
rest
above splotched yellowgreen
twisted
kneeling
bruised strawberry
and tobacco
colored
maple leaves.

Freedom Bags

(For John & Yoko)

Blue supermarket bags,
recyclable,
tumble like swarming
Portuguese man-of-war
behind our den door.
The bronze
doorknob
releases
this crushed blue
avalanche
when an empty
emerald
Australian shiraz
bottle
assaults
the bottom
of one tightly
stretched
blue
man-of-war
bag.

Maple Seeds, 2001

     Two squirrels drop maple seeds on
me right and left. One large nest above me,
plus one ample nest ten o'clock left.
The squirrels chatter, puff their tails,
and investigate every
grain of nourishment along the festive branches
of this lusty maple.

     They shower me with late
Autumn gifts,
ribbed pods
that resemble the primordial ashes
of our ancestors
now covering
the dirt floor
of this poem.

Dusk

Silverblack tail twitches
on overhead
elephant branch.

Maple seeds helicopter
like copper finches
through my fading
green thoughts.

Reisterstown, October, 2001

It's autumn dusk,
sunlight
a slab of butter.

This skin
of Friday afternoon,
chilly,
covered
with scales
sloughed
at fish markets
from Maine
to Maryland.

Halloween, 2001

To fly in a jetliner
tonight has to feel
like traveling inside the body
of an Africanized bee.

The streetlamp,
waist-deep in rose bushes,
discards a white petal
for every suffering dog
past nine PM.

Witches stroll arm in arm
below a jetliner buzzing
at ten-thousand feet
and pass the streetlamp's fallen petals.

These witches spend most of their
time in semi-darkness, splotches
of lamplight fallen like lemon peels
into their thick, smoky hair. These witches,
forever on the move, secretly protecting
our neighborhoods.

October Dogs

Neighborhood dogs
wander across fences
with antler barks
and splintered howls.

Silver chains
slide from their shiny necks
into moonlit pools
of black water.

The Old Toad

This old toad
spotted me
couple nights ago
returning
from recycling bottles and aluminum cans
at the curb.

He thought he could
imitate a rock,
but I knew
it was him,
shoulders
wrinkled
above his muscular, gold-speckled back.

Distracted, I
swiveled my head
briefly
toward a
snap of twigs
in thick, October darkness.

But when I swiveled
back,
I noticed
that my dear old friend
had quietly
relocated himself
entirely
inside
a pitch-black shadow

just below
the patio lattice.

A Storm Brewing

This storm from the Great Lakes
thickens ink
that spurts
from my squid soul
as I dive
below the depths.

I drag ink across this paper:
feathered chameleon footprints
across Florida white sand
(as opposed to thick-ridged
government issue footsteps
on the lunar surface).

Half an hour later,
the wind cultivates deep arroyos
over my footsteps.

Then the storm
swoops down
like a sperm whale
several miles
below sunlight.

Cuts me in half
at the waist.

Bouviers

Our three herding dogs
tell the boys
on the other side
of a split-rail fence
it's high time
to reconsider
their annoying behavior.

As adolescent
yelling and banging
of maple sticks
against the cobblestone driveway
gradually subsides,
only the occasional bark
is required
to cultivate the herd.

Tuesday Before Thanksgiving

Lucifer
  relaxes
 over
    my right
       shoulder.

A carnation
   for
      your soul
  he
    whispers
      to the
            swan-
         neck
       faucet
  poised above
         my
      stainless
              steel
        kitchen
           sink.

The swan-neck
      faucet
  squeezes
       my reflection,
     elongates
         it like
         a
       torn
          &

40

                              bruised
        El Greco
                    cloud.

Palomino Leaves

Elements
crushed
by a red November wind:
twisted, wild
and curled
palomino leaves.

Dogs tapping
their opaque claws
upon these leaves
chilled by Canadian air
leave yellow footprints
in my blood.

Solitude

Wine's black hips slosh a pale, blood-stained carnation.

Napkins scattered like poker chips across the Formica
table.

An ebony violin guides a blind and arthritic Peruvian
jaguar
on a silken chain past our wheezy refrigerator.

Thanksgiving Eve

A penny
          for your guilt.

     I'm collecting
               for the poor.

          A nickel
                    still buys a pint of blood
               in Northern Ireland.

Part III

The Holy One disguised as an old person
In a cheap hotel
Goes out to beg for carfare.
But I never seem to catch sight of him.
If I did, what would I ask him?
He has already experienced what is missing in my life.

--Kabir

The Day Alice Came by

Alice invited herself
for tea;
she's like that.

The eight of clubs,
tired of being
drowned
alongside
wildebeest, lioness, and zebra
in the crocodile's river of knowledge,
politely doffed his felt fedora
then scurried off to lunch.

That left me alone with Alice.

We talked about Goya,
then pondered how certain thoughts
often resemble sculpture
and architecture,
a la Calder,
until, suddenly, stray bullets
began streaking like rays of sunlight
through warped wallboards in the afterworld.

These bullets
of sunlight
were heading straight for us!

Alice took another pill.

I dissolved in moonlight
somewhere around Glyndon Drive.

Wednesday

The afternoon sun
drags her dirty-blond hair
across our kitchen table.

The late hour, a flock of starlings
blown like pepper
this way
and that.

November circles the house
in a burning red costume
designed to fool death.

Sundown

Do you crave a coquina
ebbed waist-deep
in the Gulf's glistening
black sand?

The coquina's pulse
is weak.

Or would you prefer
to lie
suspended in a hammock,
a cocoon of sorts,
both ends notched
to the infinite?

A puzzle that requires no resolution?

Wait! I've got it!
I'll bet what you really crave are those exhausted
salmon muscles just beginning
to sag along the old arm bones
of the dusking sky.

Or are you simply,
hopelessly, predisposed,
indefatigably infatuated
with a simple
dark-waisted coquina
half-sunk
in the glistening Gulf?

The Day After

A woman's transparent eyes the color
of mantis eyes.

Pupils, tiny black seeds
at the center of pale jade.

Eyebrow twitches;
a flock of starlings sweeps sideways
as November exhales.

Dusk crosses her blue legs
nearby
in a white lawn chair.

Dusk doesn't say a word
as she glances across
the yellow eyelashes
of flowing broccoli.

Holiday from Teaching

Green castanets
spill over the sunken backs
of the horses of instruction.

So, today, these horses
reject their bureaucratic loads of hay,
reject their chrome blinders
riveted to harnesses of conventional wisdom.

Today, these sad horses,
almost as heavy as their precious enigmatic
tornadoes of jealousy,
arise
on weightless hooves
to look at the world
through the wild, clear eyes of joy!

Capers

Capers
were about the size
I was looking for.

Their bitterness,
sublime,
undressed my tongue.

My Companion and I Listen to Paco de Lucia
Play *Solo Quiero Caminar*

The guitar note
bends
with ease
like a green thorn
beneath my bare foot.

Seeking my fatal flaw,
another guitar note,
a brittle thorn,
dives
through our entwined sensibilities.

A sinew
or a rusted
spring in your backbone
pulls away
from muscle.

I watch you
windblown
creak to and fro
like a whitewashed screen door
on a Georgia farmhouse porch.

Childhood

(For Rusty McClain)

Hanging in the closets
of childhood
were secrets
followed by
embarrassments,
and small hand guns,
bluejays
of injustice
cocked
against cool darkness.

And just below the sweatshirt
not worn
in weeks
slept
the pearl-handled
egalitarian life
you were promised.

As anxiety
carved your
adolescent
grief,
each dawn
you arose
an outcast Phoenix
from the ashes
of your dreams.

November 30, 2001

George Harrison died on a blue moon.

A man wanders down our neighborhood sidewalk
beneath a mercury vapor streetlamp tonight.

One side jaundiced, the other side blue.

Not so much the streetlamp, I mean, as the aureole
orbiting the stranger's solitude.

November Morning

The coffee
steps out
of her Peruvian bean,
shivers
her mink feathers
in the cold.

The pink carnation,
humanity
disheveled to one side
of her face,
rouge
indiscriminately applied,
leans forward
like an exotic bird
or terrestrial saint,
a religion
of dried blood
like exhausted mascara
dusting the petals
above her eyes.

On Dealing with Fate

It's like you're holding a poker hand
when fate suddenly snatches
your wild card,
and there's nothing
you can do about it!

So, right then,
slip into your most comfortable
skin,
whether naked
or drenched
in fireplace light licking a champagne glass
causing you to resemble
a healthy young jaguar,
and cinch your soul
tightly above despair.

Next, I would invite this fate
over for a meal
consisting of mango, pistachio, Swiss chocolates,
and heavily-doctored Jamaican coffee.

Then quickly press
your warm, quivering lips
against fate's humid waist.

This is no time
to be coy!

Coral Voice

When you have the ocean,
a coral voice
sweeps you
beneath a handful of currents.

Though drowning in the temporal ocean,
still you're awash
in green and ivory
teeth and tongues.

But when you have the ocean,
you have plenty of time: weeks, months,
years, maybe, like a rhetorical pilgrimage of monks
across volcanic mountains of grief.

On the other hand, the coral voice
also resembles white sand,
that god, in his infinite wisdom,
has chosen to blow across your naked feet.

November Love Poem

The harmonica is a young evangelist
just fallen
in love with a gypsy.

The gypsy is a garter snake
with hair and fingernails
of green fire
devouring large, festive dreams.

Each gypsy scale…a reed on the harmonica.

All colors, starting with bruised mango,
flow from the gypsy's hungry lips.

Blinded by love,
the harmonica
now recognizes the universe
as various colors:
assaulted amethyst, guava, and lemon sawgrasses
hidden
among the yellow sands
of despair.

Love Poem

I inhale the carnation,
her face
a hint
of intelligent rouge.

My shoulders
collapse
like old pigeon bones
on the wire roost
of a tarpapered
tenement roof
in the Bronx.

Listening to Roy Buchanan's *Peter Gunn*

Roy Buchanan's reptilian telecaster
claws azalea wallpaper from the graveyard
of us poor mortals still alive.

God always demands our love,
or the universe,
whichever comes first.

Tragic Hero

When the chair
turns into a dog,
a discarded dog
like the one Caesar
kicked aside
just hours
before his death,
a dog
with a collar
of magnesium,
a dog
wearing the ragged mask
of a blind
soothsayer.

When this chair
oozes
droplets of blood
from its wooden legs,
and sun's rays
like termites
chew
the husk
of your
daily existence.

On this day,
I recommend
feigning
illness,
and swallowing

melancholy
dreams
below a
muscular thunder
that rattles the terracotta
ceiling
of another man's
fate.

Dream that Includes a Painting by Michael Parkes

She cinches her innocence
at the hip
and blows large bubbles,
just as a silver, marble, man-lion
stretches for the farthest bubble.

It could be a blazing moon
rising
on the other side
of this silver, marble, man-lion's
insidious madness.

On the other hand,
your ancestors,
none of whom
look
the least bit familiar,
line up
one by one
to watch
white rainbows dissolve
on the naked waist
of the farthest glowing bubble.

It was dead clear
to our superstitious ancestors
that this one, single,
glowing bubble
was the miracle
they'd been waiting for
all their lives.

Part IV

*…He was, undoubtedly, one of those
ordinary rationalists who could not rise
to the logic of the Absurd.*

--Charles Baudelaire

Another Evening, Possibly in December, as I Recall

An old black Bouvier staggers
up cement steps
covered
with worn artificial
green turf.

Above Shasta's grunts,
the iron railing
breathes a sigh
of rust and relief.

Yellow porch light.

A motorcycle,
abdomen
of bees,
cruises by
carrying the rare blue moon
in its side pouch.

Chrome studs
on the black sky
vibrate loose
as neighborhood dogs
splinter the icy darkness.

Christmas, 2001

Your heartbeat, rhetorical,
like Shakespeare's dialogue.

A fat turkey hisses
on the grill.

December Sun

The afternoon sun descends
until I notice the fuzz
on my nose.

Intrigued as I am
about infinite possibilities
and shamans
incubating
the bridge
of my nose,
I remain, however,
equally fascinated
by shadows
that resemble muscles
hanging
then oozing
like ocelots
through the patio lattice.

Barbequing, Christmas, 2001

The tongs,
bowlegged
like a Bolivian grandmother
shouldering clay jugs
from the river.

The propane tank
spattered
with psychedelic
rusted
free-roaming
tears.

Disintegrated, black grills
lean against
a carport brace,
sadly recalling
the glorious salmon
and squash days
of summer.

December, 2001

Exhale more than you inhale.

Two or three times,
to make sure
you get it right.

Now swivel
your fountain
stool
in December's
black throat;
a month
of explosive neon
or arbitrary death?

Purple robes
refract
moonlight
that vaporizes
fingertips
on the flesh
of our
affordable gods.

Happy Holidays!

Saxophone's French braids…
champagne curls
flooding deep hollows
along December's smooth neck.

Silence inside my hands
…deafening.

Four Birds

Raven, with a galvanized
washboard, glides above
a blue spruce.

Ford pick-up drags its disintegrated muffler,
lawn mowers, hedge clippers and rakes
slowly past our house.

Yellow finches flicker the jade pines.

Two female cardinals resemble
brass smoke rings.

Driftwood-colored warbler
shatters
the glass sky.

Ode to Ether

(I hung my head.)
        --Sting

Sullen brown hair,
once a border
for Montana
blue eyes,
now tattered
by aluminum winds
crossing vast plains
enroute
to a neon cocktail glass
rocking
above
a Miami Beach nightclub.

Sullen brown hair
ripples and resembles
ultraviolet vibrations
on the black and gold
drone strings
of Sting's bass guitar.

Despair,
each feather
a bruised heartbeat.

Pour it
into a song,
or this poem.
Balance it

on the razored antlers
of brain cells,
if you prefer.

It'll etherize
into words,
anyway.

Green Oxygen

The ocean was eccentric,
the white Australian wine eccentric,
and public education,
in its fashion.

The search for truth
in the *Bible*,
definitely eccentric.

But the world spins
on its axis, anyway,
a universe
of junk:
moons melted
beside candle flames,
and hope,
a scantily-feathered green parrot
perched and shivering
inside its cylindrical, black cage.

So, the question remains:
Can you bathe yourself
in a river of excrement and ox urine
and still devote every silk
corolla of available love
to green oxygen?

Well...I suppose,
and perhaps
at the exact moment
Westminster Chimes

from a kitchen wall clock
spray
poinsettia leaves
with German brass bells trapped
between the casual folds
of thirsty red tongues.

But...what about the ocean?
What about the wine
and Walt Whitman's robust intellectuals
dented and bruised
beyond civil recognition?

What about truth,
a warm-blooded truth
that rubs
ankles
and purrs
and peels with
raspy tongue
each green feather
from the shivering body of hope?

Indeed, what about refugees
bathing in a river
polluted
by ignorance
and despair,
rinsing their silken blueblack hair
made of crows
in the indefatigably
shivering body of love?
Yes. All refugees flee
their volcanic homes,

eventually,
refugees of love and hope.

But what about the saddest
lovers of all:
You and me?

Late Afternoon Wine

Sunlight
           ignites
    a drop
  of merlot
         shivering
    on the lips
of a
    cold
      afternoon.

Diminutive sun
    blazes
   a heartbeat
      on the
    swollen
     waist
        of this
  crystal
    wine glass.

March Afternoon

An early afternoon mourning dove
devours a school bus
...an empty, yellow, woolly caterpillar
with black spots
behind its fuzzy head.

A male cardinal's
sharp whistles
sound like
raindrops
overflowing a galvanized bucket.

An orange cardinal,
smoky mask,
smoky shoulders,
sends spirals of mercury
around the bare arms
of a winter maple.

A siren pulses
a side street,
an aneurysm
in this otherwise pleasant
early March
afternoon,
as steady
Tai Chi light
coerces black diamonds
through the patio lattice.

Friday, March 8, 2002

A dried magnolia leaf
scuttles our carport
like a horseshoe crab.

Skittling her tiny points
of existence
across our chilly March patio.

But this magnolia leaf is already ancient,
several days ahead
of new buds
still bathing their beautiful roots
of amnesia
in utter darkness.

And, again, this
magnolia leaf
scuttles sideways,
tapping her jade fingernails
against the iridescent windows
of my thoughts.

March Dream

(For Vaslov Najinski)

When a cyclone devours a pink, stucco house,
when a water-stained brown finch
sings from the spine of a blue spruce,
when the cardinal's hypodermic
drops of quicksilver
drip down
the sides of a burning
calendar
made from advertising waxes.

When robins and mockingbirds
mop
the late afternoon's
forehead
with silk handkerchiefs
woven from the abandoned skins
of reptilian oboes.

They dominate
when the air
turns blue!

They dominate
the walnut hair
of winter hedges,
and the husks
of yellow squash
abandoned
like coyote skulls

and Mescalero dreams
along the surface
of gravity.

When crows
drag their souls
of Cuban cigars
beneath maple branches
bored like the black-gloved fingertips
of a Prime Minister's mistress
draped across the shoulders of my split-rail fence.

When
frozen barks
from woolly black dogs
disturb
nests
of twilight
dripping from the thoughts
of the prisoner.

The thoughts' antlers
graze on gray air.

Squirrels
and the occasional topaz chirp
of a northeastern sparrow
whose tiny tusks
of rubber and steel
plow fresh veins
through our
gas grill
love affairs.

When driftwood
unhooks a black telephone
from the ocean,
curls of foam
unfurl the scattered bones
of religious terrorists
washed up on the shores
of dementia.

David lays down his sling
to fold freshly laundered, white napkins
on the humid patio
of the Breakers Hotel.

At this precise moment,
the Lake Worth pier
exposes her waist
of amnesia.

When the wheels of injustice
creak
below balconies' moonlight
igniting white flour
fingerprints
of popes, governors, dictators
and other rented security forces.

When the wind
rips the flesh of sentimental blue
from the spectrum,
turning it inside
out revealing
intestines
the color

of Irish whiskey.

Shadows fall
from maple trees
leaving large, permanent stains
on my thighs.

A faun
rustles
the maple seed
inside my chest.

House Finches

House finches, two of them,
have adopted
this ornamental porcelain
bird house
hanging by a thin chain
outside our back door.

She has the most gorgeous
coriander feathers,
eyes
two drops of black oil.

Her mate fluffs
his vermilion shoulders
of smoldering
coals.

It's late March,
early cardinals whistle
in loops
of water.

April Dusk

Saber teeth
sunlight
splinter the lattice.

Long shadows,
slugs migrating the red torso
of silence.

Blue jays
cry
like flint.

Mockingbirds create
a chorus
of orchids
and switchblades.

Dark Matter

(Understanding something you cannot see is difficult – but not impossible. Not surprisingly, astronomers currently study dark matter by its effects on the bright matter that we do observe. For instance, when we watch a nearby star wobbling predictably, we infer from calculations that a 'dark planet' orbits around it.)

--Vera Rubin

The poet
sees dark matter at the bottom
of his wine glass.

Near the bottom of the glass,
he sees Magdalena's swirling waist of gravity
filled with the smoke of dark matter.

And Magdalena's eyes
of dark matter.

He knows all the vowels of bamboo that click
in a green wind blowing through Magdalena's voice
once grew in the thick, fertile soil of dark matter.

He touches Magdalena's hair,
flowing dark matter.

All the bassoons, oboes, and cellos
that orbit Magdalena's humid hips,
ah, create the irresistible pulse
of dark matter.

The poet enjoys the last drops
of dark matter

rolling like sweat
down Magdalena's glass waist.

Gray April

So, I guess that's the danger
of moving too slowly.

Pretty soon, inertia.

A leopard slug
grazes on algae.

Black stones
rattle
a cardinal's beak.

Using zero as a reference.

Lime green
maple
embryos.

April Birds

A finch's neck
the color of rhubarb.

A sparrow taps
tin melancholy.

A goldfinch
warbles
then empties her pockets;
silver and bronze
foreign coins
cascade her feet.

Cockatiel

This thin-shouldered
snow-white cockatiel in a Cocoa Beach
thatched restaurant
announced
scrambled eggs,
blintzes,
plus pink and green melon
with strawberries
and cloudy grapes
all tossed
into a large parquet bowl.

Just beyond the faded, coral-colored wall,
the ocean's green hair
dragged its white knuckles across blond sand.

Every morning without fail,
the cockatiel acknowledged the entrance of every
    tourist
poorly disguised by sunburn and madras shorts.

Behind his thin bars
of faith
he lived
to be a very old bird.

Birds of the Universe Congregate in Reisterstown

Chirps and whistles
wear straw hats
made in Bogotá.

The orange cardinal's loop
inside a bright green maple
is a political statement
pertaining
to the Middle East
or Central America,
whichever culture
is most vulnerable
at any given moment.

Finches nest
for the next three hundred years
in an industry-woven
shadow-eaten
machinegun-beaten
straw hat.

Curious Universe

If I could be carried
like mulch
in a crow's beak,
or drip like quicksilver
from a starling's beak
onto the low branch
of a blue spruce,
this April breeze
would devour me.

Gladly, I'd consider everything
this stage in life
to be the rare sensibility
of purple orchids
curling their ivory bones
around our curious universe.

According to Gospel

We can't even see past these hedges
of spring —
forsythia
dominating early signs
of rose-of-Sharon's
lavender hips.

But Sharon's luscious aureoles
could kill us,
we're told,
if we
perceive the universe
with impure intention,
so sayeth our gospel fathers.

April Afternoon

Dog legs
flicker lattice;
Jacques' vermilion collar
alerts the aureole
orbiting
the robin's
dazzling green overture.

The robin
braids her song
around a thick gray maple branch.

Her song, a small garter snake
disguised as an asp
escaping
the golden cup
of truth.

Part V

Outside, it is still the time
Of suffering before the image.
In the closed hand of the outside
The wheat of things of the world
Begins to sprout.

--Yves Bonnefoy

Solitude in a Park in Thurmont, Maryland

A tiny bird, iridescent night blue, visits a hole inside
a large knot on the lower trunk of a poplar. He returns to
that hole; darts inside four or five seconds, then emerges
to streak away, each time in a new direction, bouncing on
currents of air at the speed of an arrow. Upon returning,
to feed his mate no doubt, he lands upon the swollen
knuckle of that poplar, tail down, head straight up like a
compass needle, gripping the wrinkled gray bark that
resembles an elephant's leg. He leaps inside, departs,
then returns again, again, and again. Eventually, I can
bear it no longer and, finally, upon one of his many
returns he finds me inside that smoky shadow on the
swollen knuckle of the poplar, soul wide open, ecstatic!

An Early, California Merlot

This merlot is like a wild quarter horse
from Montana,
spirited,
but not
all that ready
to settle down.

Fortunately, unlike the culture
that delivers
tragic nightmares
and other catastrophic events
via 50-caliber rounds
and night-vision, nuclear tanks,
young wine
sleeps
soundly
in its oak
barrel
of amnesia.

William Blake

William Blake is the fountain.

Of course, there are tributaries
to Blake: Milton, Donne, Marvell, etc.

But Blake set the standard
for poems
to rise up
on their hind legs
and shred fate
with their
scissored forearms
flared like two golden jumping spiders
on a mango leaf.

Blake believed that thoughts
were organic,
had flavor,
like plums crushed
into madness
and despair.

He ate philosophies
like a sandwich,
with apologies
overflowing the sides
as scraps of thought
dangling
just beyond
our imaginations.

May Dusk

The dog's ears,
dark flames.

Not the fire,
surely,
but angry
smoke that spirals
from the tips
of burning leaves.

A large black ant
circles
a crystal boot
half-filled with topaz ale
on our picnic table.

The ant
scales
a gardening glove's
petrified
glistening
black holes
for fingertips,
then traverses
many rivers
of blue ink,
across galaxies
infinitely small and large,
leaving behind
tiny pawprints
on his journey

through the thick,
sleepy jungle
of my humid poem.

Monday Evening

Maples hiss
when a May wind
rubs her hips
against their thick
green leaves.

Every bird in the neighborhood:
springs winding,
metaphysical pulleys in need
of religious oil,
melodic rivers
flowing past thin reeds,
all weightless
as Mozart flutes.

The Ant

Wind flares the ant's bronze tentacles.

Suddenly, the ant's glistening universe
struggles
with moments
of lost control.

This ant will experience many
such
moments
during his
short weeks of existence.

But today
he seems quite content
to roam
the blackened edge
of an old picnic board
lying on its stomach
in the thick ashes
of late spring mockingbirds.

After a Storm

Green smoke
licks the muscular ribs
of an algae-covered, split-rail fence.

Finches,
slashes of white
across their foreheads,
sharpen their
lexicons
against the feathery branches
of a giant blue spruce.

Humidity's
fingertips
warm the pulse
against my neck.

Wild Parrots

When wild parrots emerged,
they were a lively exchange
of brass and silver
beneath the canopy
of the Amazon.

But slowly as Euro coins
clinked into a pile,
a pile of rising smoke,
a pile of crushed bones
once attached to green muscle,
all this chattering of fowl dominance
and parrot responsibility
faded into corroded squawks
now lying at the bottom
of a rainbow-colored,
indoor, Palm Beach Gardens
shopping mall fountain.

Thoreau Says We Must Live Within Two Miles of Our Primary Childhood

I sleep.

Alarm clock's
green antlers
tear holes
in my significant dream
as solid as a wild mustang
of dry Arizona wind.

Raindrops splatter
like hollow, red,
shotgun cartridges.

Sleet hisses.

Spring's Interference

Amidst a vast chorus of bird songs, tonight,
only the mockingbird's willing
to drag down
the walls of faith
like Samson.

Mockingbird,
tonight,
lightning flashes
across wings
of gunmetal gray,
advances
our morality,
despite bulldozers
grazing in large herds
the ashes
of the Twin Towers.

Love Poem

Crows wear loose-fitting attitudes
that fall like black tarps
over the spring order of things.

I've heard that lament before,
but like the horsefly
bugging heaven,
I confess
to ignorance
when it comes
to nagging questions of love.

New love,
like adolescent geometry,
dips its faith
into the pool of illusion.

Twilight

Robins announce darkness.

Punctuated by blue jays
on a rusted porch swing.

A manatee sheds its skin
and that's dusk.

Bitten

Once bitten by the brown recluse god,
you suffer
intensely.

You struggle,
but freedom
is a lock
whose key
lies hidden in a safe
guarded by the sales department
wearing long flowing robes
of black water.

Deacons, like waiters,
balance
collection plates
full of green salads:
fortunes,
or lies,
broadcast
across generations
of innocence.

The recluse god
appears
quite innocent
so as
not
to disturb
the harmony
of greedy bells

tolling the distance.

But, ultimately,
when you awaken,
you'll realize
you exist
merely as a finger
waving
at heaven.

After all,
whose life is it,
anyway?

In the end,
there is no assurance
that our souls
are woven from steel and orchids
or that some souls
are destined
to fly
like ragged strands of geese
across a winter landscape
of intelligence.

A Rainy Thursday Afternoon

(In raising a child, or a dog, discipline should never mean
a withholding of love.)
                    --Chanelle Britt

Chanelle thinks of this on our way
to the J to deliver
Chelsea's forgotten membership card.

As we idle silver puddles,
the red
of a traffic light
ripples
their surface,
then a yellow
swallowtail
slowly migrates
a black puddle.

Until, finally, the green says,
I love you.
I've always loved you,
and always will.

Rattan Fans Circle the Ceiling

Her Rococo smile
retains the
dissonance
of pampered violins.

Monsoon rain
darkens her linen shoulders
and glistens
the black street.

White Thursday

It's the air.

The skin of hippo or zebra
(whichever desires wet maples the most)
gurgles the gutters
of a White Thursday.

It's early summer.

A herd of purple crows
migrates
your eyelashes.

Your taut muscles
(as Mary Magdalene
rises up before you)
release
their linen robes
of absolute joy!

Summer Love Poem

I savor
the mockingbird's limp bag
of coins:
foreign metals
with alloys
rubbing smooth hips against copper.

Ribbons swirl
as an alchemist
braids the long silver hair
of summer dusk.

Venus
peers from behind the cattails,
then oozes
like a croc
beneath my green memory.

Chilly Summer Dusk

One hopes, of course,
that it's merely
a bit of cork
floating over the chilly waves
of my late afternoon chardonnay.

Who would've guessed
that embroidered plums
across your warm linen waist
could disturb the universe
or that tarantula rain could erase
everything from previous memory?

White wine,
on a particularly cool, summer evening,
softly stumbles into the room,
our room, motionless,
that now glistens
like a scarab
at dead midnight.

June Evening

You untangle
like an octopus
slow motion
in an earthquake.

The shower's coral tiles
glisten beaded tendons
against your neck
and mirror your irrational fears.

So, now,
I suppose fears, as long as they're old,
sometimes dry and crack
into corpses like those
on daytime TV dramas?

You were victorious once,
in a game that involved
jellyfish logic;
you believed the rustling
of thick, summer maples
would guide you
through the gates of hell
and into the beautiful claws
of yet another summer rain shower
tapping the
corrugated
tin roof
of love.

Poems in Progress

You know, after abusing
these damn things,
some wounded, gashed, bleeding,
and holding their sides,
it's a wonder they trust me
at all to approach them,
considering their fragile conditions.

But I coax them,
time and time again,
urging them to reveal themselves,
cultivating generations
in their dark barrels,
knowing that any moment
could be my last.

Here's to Writing a Poem on the 13TH of Every Month for an Entire Year, but Knowing I'd Never Remember All That...

(For Carl Jung)

Taboos are like bongos;
you find the beat
you like the most,
then discard the rest
in a pawn shop
on Greenmount Avenue,
hoping they'll materialize
into beautiful rivers
on a Baltimore Araber's ebony face.

Taboos were always meant to sprout black pearls
deep in the fertile souls
of humans.

All this elaborate masquerading of taboos
typically makes me hungry
and encourages my soul
to resemble a barracuda
trolling the dark shifting floor
of our mythical collective unconscious.

José Rodeiro (Cover painting: *9/11*)

José Rodeiro is a Professor of Art and Art History, New Jersey City University (Jersey City, NJ); a Visual Artist's Fellow in Painting of the National Endowment for the Arts; a Fulbright Fellow, a Fellow of the Institute for International Education and a Cintas Fellow in painting. He received his M.F.A from Pratt Institute, NY and his Ph.D. from Ohio University's College of Fine Arts. He has lived and worked in Spain, Central America, and Latin America. He has received major public art (mural) commissions from Tampa Arts Council, Tampa, FL, and Maryland State Arts Council, Baltimore, MD. His exhibitions include the Washington County Museum of Fine Arts, Hagerstown, Maryland; Mason Gross Gallery, Rutgers University, NJ; Kenkelaba Gallery (New York State Arts Council) NYC, NY; Florida International Museum (Miami, FL), The Korea Gallery (NYC, NY), Newark Museum; NJPAC; UMDNJ's Robert Wood Johnson Gallery; Perth Amboy Gallery (Center for the Arts); La Ruche Art Consortium; PCCC Broadway/LRC Gallery (Paterson, NJ), Therese A. Maloney Art Gallery (College of Saint Elizabeth, Morristown, NJ), Qbava Gallery (Union City, NJ) and other venues. In October 2009, Rodeiro lectured on his painting *9/11* at The Tribute WTC Visitor Center (at Ground Zero, New York City, NY).

Since the 1980s, Rodeiro often educes images from two sources: his effulgent imagination and from art history. For example, Rodeiro conceived a large painting dedicated to the victims of the September 11, 2001, terrorist attack. In Rodeiro's **9/11**, *there are allusions to images found in Picasso's* **Guernica** *(1937), as well as Tarot card symbols and references to ancient Cretan labyrinthic mythology. As in* **Guernica**, *noticeable motifs of death, tragedy, and conflict prevail; these virulent elements are appropriated as symbols of a contemporary massacre. By clearly referencing Picasso's modern masterpiece (which protested an unjust, Fascist, air bombardment of innocent civilians during the Spanish Civil War), Rodeiro directly examines a day of deadly horror and loss of life that has cast a malignant specter on current world events.* (Midori Yoshimoto, <u>Neo-Latino Catalog</u>, Perth Amboy Gallery Publication, Perth Amboy, NJ: 2004.)

José Rodeiro: **www.rodeiro-art.com**

Alan Britt

Alan Britt's previous books are *Greatest Hits* (2010), *Hurricane* (2010), *Vegetable Love* (2009), *Vermilion* (2006), *Infinite Days* (2003), *Amnesia Tango* (1998), *Bodies of Lightning* (1995), *The Afternoon of the Light* (1981), *I Suppose the Darkness Is Ours* (1977), *Ashes in the Flesh* (1976); and *I Ask for Silence, Also* (1969). Essays recently in *Clay Palm Review* and *Arson*. Interviews and poetry in *Steaua* (Romania), *Latino Stuff Review* and *Poet's Market*. Other poems (selected) in *Agni, The Bitter Oleander, Bolts of Silk* (Scotland), *Christian Science Monitor, Cider Press Review, Cold Mountain Review, The Cultural Journal, English Journal, Epoch, Fire* (UK), *Flint Hills Review, Fox Cry Review, Gradiva* (Italy), *Greensboro Review, Hecale* (UK), *Kansas Quarterly, Karamu, The Kerf, Magyar Naplo* (Hungary), *Meridian Anthology of Contemporary Poetry, Midwest Quarterly, New Letters, Pacific Review, Pedrada Zurda* (Ecuador), *Puerto del Sol, Queen's Quarterly* (Canada), *Revista Solar* (Mexico), *Rosebud, Second Aeon* (Wales), *Sou'wester, Square Lake, Strangeroad, Writers' Journal,* plus the anthologies (selected): *The Poet's Cookbook: 33 American Poets with German Translations,* Forest Woods Media Productions/Goethe Institute, Washington, DC, 2010; *American Poets Against the War,* Metropolitan Arts Press, Ltd., Chicago/Athens/Dublin, 2009; *Vapor transatlántico (Transatlantic Steamer),* bi-lingual anthology of Latin American and North American poets, Hofstra University Press/Fondo de Cultura Económica de Mexico/Universidad Nacional Mayor de San Marcos de Peru, 2008; *La Adelfa Amarga: Seis Poetas Norteamericanos de Hoy,* Ediciones El Santo Oficio, Peru, 2003. *Weavings 2000: The Maryland Millennial Anthology,* Forest Woods Media Productions, Inc., Saint Mary's College, MD, 2001, and *Fathers: Poems About Fathers,* St. Martin's Press, 1998.

ABC Radio National (Australian Broadcasting Corporation) in July, 2008, broadcasted a straight read, plus live stream on their website of Alan Britt's poem, "After Spending All Day at the National Gallery," as part of their Poets on Painters series.

Alan received his Masters Degree from the Writing Seminars at Johns Hopkins University. He teaches English/Creative Writing at Towson University and lives in Reisterstown, Maryland, with his wife, daughter, two Bouviers des Flandres, one Bichon Friese, and two formerly feral cats.